D0116804

This book is a gift from

My name is

I was baptized on

My godparents are

I was / will be confirmed on

"And you will receive the gift of the Holy Spirit."
–Acts 2:38

My
CONFIRMATION
BOOK

Donna-Marie Cooper O'Boyle

PARACLETE PRESS
BREWSTER, MASSACHUSETTS

2018 Fifth Printing
2017 Fourth Printing
2016 Third Printing
2014 Second Printing
2013 First Printing

My Confirmation Book

ISBN 978-1-61261-357-4

All quotations from the Holy Bible are taken from New Revised Standard Version Bible: Catholic Edition, copyright 1989, 1993, Division of Christian Education of the National Council of the Churches of Christ in the United States of America. Used by permission. All rights reserved.

The Paraclete Press name and logo (dove on cross) are trademarks of Paraclete Press, Inc.

Library of Congress Cataloging-in-Publication Data
Cooper O'Boyle, Donna-Marie.
  My confirmation book / Donna-Marie Cooper O'Boyle.
     80 pages cm
  ISBN 978-1-61261-357-4
  1. Confirmation—Catholic Church. I. Title.
  BX2210.O26 2013
  264'.02082—dc23   2012048273

10 9 8 7 6 5

Published by Paraclete Press
Brewster, Massachusetts
www.paracletepress.com
Printed in the United States of America

Dedicated lovingly to my children
Justin, Chaldea, Jessica, Joseph, and Mary-Catherine

Contents

My
CONFIRMATION
BOOK

Introduction

"Let your good Spirit lead me on a level path."
—Psalm 143:10

W hat a privilege it is to be confirmed a Catholic! The sacrament of Confirmation will bless your life with much grace and many gifts. Throughout this book, we'll look at each gift that you will receive when you are confirmed. By gifts, we don't mean money or presents, but something far more valuable—the priceless gifts that the Holy Spirit will bestow upon you which are yours to keep forever. They are: Wisdom, Understanding, Counsel, Fortitude, Knowledge, Piety, and Fear of the Lord. God wants you to share your gifts with others each day.

To show His love for us, God gives you a free will to choose. He wants you to choose to do good. The gifts of the Holy Spirit will help you to do so.

Call on the Holy Spirit often for help, strength, and inspiration.

Come Holy Spirit,
fill the hearts of your faithful and
enkindle in us the fire of your love.

Introduction

The Bible tells us:

> The spirit of the LORD shall rest upon him:
> The spirit of wisdom and understanding,
> The spirit of counsel and might,
> A spirit of knowledge and the fear of the LORD.
> —Isaiah 11:2–3

I Am a Member of the Church

"Abide in my love."
—John 15:9

It's exciting to know that the same Holy Spirit who appeared to the apostles and the Blessed Mother at Pentecost, and who is the Third Person of the Holy Trinity, is the One who will come to you when you are confirmed.

The sacrament of Confirmation is one of the three sacraments that initiate you into the Church. The other two are Baptism and the Eucharist. Baptism gives new life to your soul, the Eucharist nourishes you with Jesus's Body and Blood, and Confirmation strengthens you and brings an increase and deepening of baptismal grace.

Jesus instituted the sacraments, which he entrusted to the Church in order to bless us with his grace. Sacraments are like holy links that keep us connected with all of the members of the Church— all over the world and even those in purgatory and heaven. When you are confirmed, your bond to the Church deepens and you grow in your faith.

In the Bible we read, "Do not fear, for I have redeemed you; I have called you by name, you are mine" (Isaiah 43:1). When you were baptized and again when you are confirmed you are called by name. You will choose a saint's name for your Confirmation. Say a prayer as you choose a meaningful name.

God is calling you by name and asking you to be a light to the world in all that you do. He wants you to be a wonderful example to others about how to live a life as a Christian. Sometimes you will have chances to talk about your faith in God, and at other times you will be a Christian example simply because of the choices you make.

In 1999 in St. Louis, Missouri, Blessed Pope John Paul II spoke to young people about Jesus's words in the Bible, "You are the light of the world." He said, "Do I believe those words of Jesus in the Gospel? Jesus is calling you the light of the world. He is asking you to let your light shine before others. I know that in your hearts you want to say:

'Here I am, Lord. Here I am. I come to do your will.'
But only if you are one with Jesus can you share his
light and be a light to the world."

I R E F L E C T

Can you take some time to think about how Jesus is calling you to be a light to the world?

What can you do today to be a light to others?

I PRAY

Here I am, Lord; I come
to do your will. Help
me to be one with you.
Please shine through me
so that others will come
to know you. Amen.

TWO

Wisdom

"How much better to get wisdom than gold!"
—Proverbs 16:16

Wisdom is considered to be the greatest gift of all. Wisdom helps you to make wise choices. It helps you to think through your plans and to choose what God wants you to do—not what the world or your friends tell you to do.

You will make many decisions in your life. It's important to pause and to pray, asking God what you should do. Don't jump into something without thinking about what might happen if you do it, about whether it is a good choice, and about how it will affect others. Ask God to give you an increase of wisdom in your heart.

CHOICES

James received a new electronic game for his birthday. He showed it to his friends at school and let them play with it at lunchtime and recess. James's friend Tom asked to use it. When recess was over Tom quickly stuck the game in his backpack and ran back inside. Another of James's friends, Joseph, saw Tom put it in his backpack. Later on, James asked Tom for his game. Tom said he thought he might have left it outside. Tom had a funny feeling in his stomach because he lied about the game. James felt very sad. He had just received it from his parents for his birthday, and he was afraid it was lost. He thought his parents might be upset because he took it to school.

Joseph heard Tom tell James he didn't have the game. Joseph knew that Tom was not telling the truth. What should Joseph do? Would it be tattling to tell James? Would Tom be mad at Joseph?, he wondered.

Joseph decided to say a quiet prayer. After praying, Joseph had a strong feeling he should privately tell his teacher, Mrs. Jenkins, what happened. He realized in his heart that this wouldn't be tattling—it would be seeking truth and justice. Joseph's teacher was happy to hear from Joseph and did not tell Tom or James how she knew about the missing game. Mrs. Jenkins asked Tom to look in his backpack for James's game. After Tom pulled out the game, Mrs. Jenkins retuned it to the rightful owner—James.

In this story, James learned that he should listen to his parents and not take expensive items to school. Tom felt sorry that he lied and that he had planned to steal James's game. He confessed to Mrs. Jenkins and James, and later on, he went to Confession at the church and felt much better. Joseph felt peace in his heart because he made the wise choice by praying and following through by telling his teacher what happened.

I   REFLECT

What would you do if you were James? What if you were Tom? What if you were Joseph?

How can prayer help you to become wise and make the right decisions?

I PRAY

Dear God, please send the Holy Spirit to me to guide and inspire me to always make the right choices and do the right thing. Amen.

THREE

Understanding

*"The unfolding of your words gives light;
it imparts understanding to the simple."*
—Psalm 119:130

Understanding is a gift from the Holy Spirit
that sharpens our understanding of God
and also of other human beings. As a Catholic
Christian, you really should do your best to learn
about and understand your faith so that you can live
it properly. The Holy Spirit will help you. When

you live your faith you are being a good example to others around you who might not know God. Your good example is like a prayer for them. It's a way to shine a light in the darkness.

A PRAYERFUL EXAMPLE

Alexandra invited three of her girlfriends to her house for a birthday slumber party. It was a beautiful summer day, not too hot, but just right for a swim. After a refreshing time in the pool, the girls enjoyed pizza on the deck. Alexandra tossed a few pieces of pizza crust to her dog, Cricket, and asked her friends to join her in the screened gazebo where they would talk about girl stuff and she would open presents. The gazebo was decorated with colorful streamers and balloons.

Understanding

Soon after that, Alexandra's mother walked in carrying a beautiful birthday cake with candles all aglow. Everyone sang "Happy birthday" to Alexandra. It was fun to celebrate a birthday with friends, she thought. That evening the girls spread their sleeping bags on Alexandra's living room floor while Alexandra's dad popped a big batch of popcorn for the girls to enjoy while they watched a family movie.

Afterward, Alexandra's mom and dad took a few minutes with Alexandra to say their night prayers. Sally, one of the girlfriends, asked Alexandra what she had been doing in the kitchen with her parents. Alexandra told her that every night they say prayers together. Sally wanted to know why. She had never said prayers before. She also asked why pictures of Jesus and Mary were on the living room walls. These questions gave Alexandra a chance to share about her Catholic faith. Sally was not only curious, but she was also interested in learning more.

Since Alexandra had a very good understanding of her Catholic faith because of her upbringing and faith formation classes, she was able to be a light to Sally and her other friends by explaining what prayer is and why she prays. The next day Sally asked her parents if they would take her to church.

I REFLECT

Why is it important to stick to your prayer schedule even if you have guests? Can you think of two reasons?

If you were Alexandra, how would you explain the Catholic faith to Sally?

I PRAY

Dear Lord,
Jesus, help me to
understand my
faith even better.
Please send your
Holy Spirit to me.
Amen.

FOUR

Counsel

*"Your word is a lamp to my feet
and a light to my path."*
—Psalm 119:105

The Holy Spirit brings you the gift of Counsel when you are confirmed. This gift is important and assures you that you will be able to act correctly in times of need or trouble. Counsel helps you to be open to the inspiration and guidance of the Holy

Spirit. It helps you to think clearly and act rightly to make correct judgments promptly.

Counsel builds on the two previous gifts of Wisdom and Understanding. It also perfects the virtue of Prudence, which helps you think things through beforehand. Through the gift of Counsel the Holy Spirit enlightens a person to know what to do in specific situations that come about in daily life.

AIDING WITH COUNSEL

St. Catherine of Siena was born in 1347 in Siena, Italy. When she was only six years old she was blessed with a vision of the Blessed Mother holding the Christ Child. Through her prayers asking God what she should do with her life,

Catherine came to know that God wanted her to follow the two great commandments, which are to love God and love our neighbor. Catherine grew up to work with people in need. She tried her best to make everyone around her feel better. She possessed many gifts, which she used to help many people. God gave her the gifts of healing and of knowledge of the consciences of others, and the gift of predicting future events. Many holy people consulted with her because they knew she was holy and had a great gift of Counsel.

Through her gift of Counsel, St. Catherine even helped a pope! This was Pope Gregory XI. She worked very hard in many ways to aid the Church. We might assume that St. Catherine was able to do amazing things because she was a saint. But, truth be told, we are all called to become saints—even you! God wants you to pray often and ask for his gifts so that you too can help others and also please God.

I R E F L E C T

Can you ask God to awaken all of the gifts of the
Holy Spirit in your heart?

Think about a time you needed to make a quick
decision about something very important. Did you
pray for help from the Holy Spirit? Will you pray
next time?

I PRAY

Dear Lord, Jesus, please guide me to know what you'd like me to do with my life. Help me to help others as St. Catherine has done. Amen.

FIVE

Fortitude

"I am content with weaknesses, insults, hardships,
persecutions, and calamities for the sake of Christ;
for whenever I am weak, then I am strong."
—2 Corinthians 12:10

Fortitude gives strength to the soul. We might think of courage when we ponder the meaning of Fortitude. This gift allows us to cope with various struggles. The Christian martyrs who were willing to give their lives rather than renounce their faith in God exhibited the gift of Fortitude. But this gift can be utilized in less dramatic, but still very important ways too, each day, such as by being courageous against the evils of the world by not getting involved in them. Sometimes you'll use the gift of Fortitude when putting up with insults or unjust attacks.

HE WILL HOLD YOU UP

St. Thomas More was a strong defender of the Church, and he spent most of his life writing in defense of it. Although he was a friend of King Henry VIII and held a position as Lord Chancellor of England, St. Thomas resigned in 1532 because he couldn't recognize the king as the head of the Church in England, and he refused to compromise his religious beliefs and abide by the king's political demands. He was imprisoned in the Tower of London because of this.

St. Thomas wrote to his daughter from prison, "I will not mistrust [God] . . . though I shall feel myself weakening and on the verge of being overcome with fear. I shall remember how St. Peter at a blast of wind began to sink because of his lack of faith, and I shall do as he did: call upon Christ and pray to him for help. And then I trust he shall place his holy hand on me and in the stormy seas hold me up from drowning."

St. Thomas was tried and convicted of treason. On July 6, 1535, he told his judges he hoped they "may yet hereafter in heaven all meet together to everlasting salvation." As he was led to the scaffold to be beheaded, he told the spectators that he would die as "the king's good servant, but God's first."

Each day God gives you an opportunity to be courageous and brave as a defender of the faith. What you do in setting a good Christian example, for instance when not going along with the crowd concerning immodest clothing or watching inappropriate movies and television, may seem small or insignificant, but when done with love these things make a huge difference to God and to others.

I REFLECT

How can you defend your faith today in a charitable way?

What little act of surrender can you do today? Can you say, "no thank you" to an invitation from a peer to see an inappropriate movie or a trip to the mall where your friends might purchase items that are not favorable to a holy life?

I PRAY

Dear Lord, teach me to be always faithful to the one true King and not to the things of this world. Increase my gift of Fortitude so I will be charitable even when others ridicule or insult me. Amen.

SIX

Knowledge

*"An intelligent mind acquires knowledge,
and the ear of the wise seeks knowledge."*
—Proverbs 18:15

The gift of Knowledge allows you to see things in your life with God's purpose. You can begin to understand why God has placed you in your individual circumstances.

Knowledge helps you to become convinced about the truths of the faith and aids you to understand the difference between inspirations from God and temptations from the devil. Knowledge of your faith will help you understand more clearly how you are to live your life as a Catholic Christian.

A SHINING EXAMPLE

Christina and her twin sister Chloe were Catholics who practiced their faith with their family and attended faith formation classes at their parish. During one class the subject of heaven, hell, and purgatory was discussed. Christina raised her hand and explained that if she ever saw her twin sister falling down into hell she would run to grab her and save her.

The teacher told the student that she was pleased that she wanted to prevent her sister from going to hell. But, Mrs. Cobens told Christina and the class, there's no possible way to snatch someone from falling into hell after they die. The time to protect someone from hell, she explained, is during our lifetime. Our Christian example and our knowledge of the faith can help others in many ways.

Most of the time we do not realize the good that God is doing through us when our hearts are prayerful and faithful. But when we are one with God, our words and actions make an enormous difference to others.

I REFLECT

How can your action today help to change someone in a good way?

Can you strive to learn more about your faith? Reading the lives of the saints is both fascinating and helpful to your spiritual life.

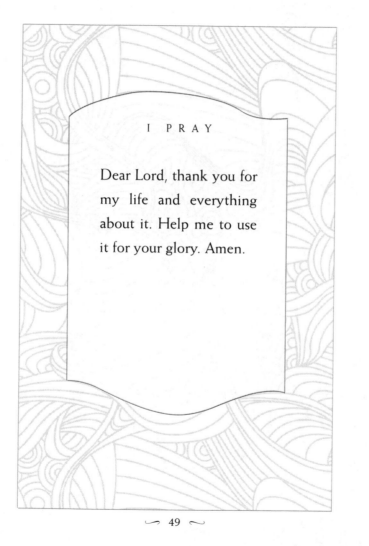

I PRAY

Dear Lord, thank you for my life and everything about it. Help me to use it for your glory. Amen.

SEVEN

Piety

*"May my meditation be pleasing to him,
for I rejoice in the LORD."*
—Psalm 104:34

Piety is a special gift from the Holy Spirit. With Piety we give honor, glory, worship, and affection to God, which he deserves from us. The gift of Piety instills an instinctive desire in us to pray and love God. It helps bring us closer to him.

Spending time with God in prayer will deepen your gift of Piety. You can keep company with

God during your personal prayers to him at home, at Mass, and while adoring Jesus in the Blessed Sacrament, and really at any time at all. Our Lord wants you to come to him often, to speak to him, and to take time to listen to him speak to your heart.

Blessed Pope John Paul II told us that with the gift of Piety, "the Spirit heals our hearts of every form of hardness, and opens them to tenderness towards God and our brothers and sisters" (Angelus, May 28, 1989).

PIETY IN ACTION

Let's consider a few scenarios. A woman is kneeling in a front pew at church, spending time with Jesus in the Blessed Sacrament. A mother brings her three children into church and they scurry over to the statues and candles in the back and kneel down to pray for a family intention. A young athlete kneels by his bed in the morning, looks at the crucifix on his wall, and asks God to help him with his upcoming soccer game. A family goes to the local diner one evening, and after they thank the waitress for bringing their meal to the table, they bow their heads, make the Sign of the Cross, and say their Grace Before Meals prayer.

Which person or people in the four scenes above are using the gift of Piety? Indeed, they all are. It's good to know that we can pray at anytime and anywhere, even if there are rules about not praying (such as in school). In reality, no rule can ever stop you from silently retreating to your heart in prayer. No one will know you are praying, except God, Mary, the angels, and the saints. God wants you to think of him often and to go to him with all your needs.

I REFLECT

In what ways can you spend more time with God in prayer?

Can you cut back on some television, electronic games, or Internet use, in order to make more time for God?

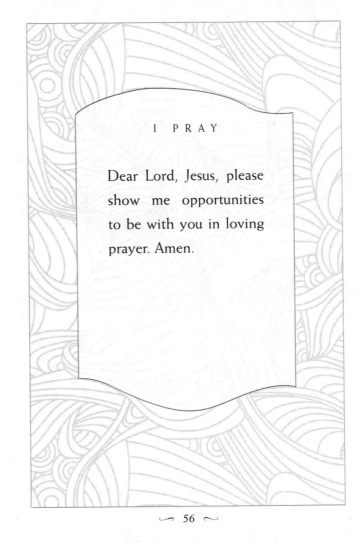

I PRAY

Dear Lord, Jesus, please show me opportunities to be with you in loving prayer. Amen.

EIGHT

Fear of the Lord

"The fear of the LORD is the beginning of wisdom,
and the knowledge of the
Holy One is insight."
—Proverbs 9:10

The Holy Spirit gives you the gift of the Fear of the Lord. This does not mean that you run in fear from God, but rather that you sincerely reverence the Lord because he is God. You will want to live your life in accordance with God's laws, which he gives us to help us get to heaven and so that we won't go to hell.

Because there are bad things in the world that can be very distracting as well as tempting, and because the advertising industry is expert at selling so many things that can take you away from God, you must stand firm in your faith and in your Fear of the Lord. Fear God so that you will love him. Then you will know that each day of your life you are working on your final reward of Everlasting Life of happiness with God.

Will you choose to stay on the right path through life and be rewarded eternal happiness with God in heaven? Or will you allow the culture to tell you how to live your life? The choice is yours.

The Holy Spirit is always ready and nearby waiting to help you with all of your decisions. Don't forget to ask for help when you pray.

I   REFLECT

Psalm 34:8–9 says this: "O taste and see that the LORD is good; happy are those who take refuge in him. O fear the LORD, you his holy ones, for those who fear him have no want." What do you think these verses mean?

How can you be an example to others so that they will be helped to come closer to God?

I PRAY

Dear Lord, Jesus, thank
you for this gift of the
Holy Spirit so that I can
be mindful of all of my
decisions in life. Amen.

NINE

I Am a Light to the World!

"You are the light of the world. . . .
[L]et your light shine
before others, so that they may
see your good works and give
glory to your Father in heaven."
—Matthew 5:14, 16

The sacrament of Confirmation gives you so many wonderful gifts, graces, and blessings. As sacramental grace grows in your life you may feel a spiritual awakening in your heart and soul.

By praying each day, you will indeed grow in faith, hope, and love. Always remember: your life of holiness can be like a shining torch that can help draw many others to Christ's love. Don't be afraid to show God's love to others.

As Blessed Mother Teresa of Calcutta once said, "Not all of us can do great things, but we can do small things with great love."

"Are you ready for this?" Blessed Pope John Paul II asked, when he spoke to young people in St. Louis in 1999. "Because Jesus is the Light, we, too, become light when we proclaim him. This is the heart of the Christian mission to which each of you are called through Baptism and Confirmation. You are called to make the light of Christ shine brightly in the world."

Are you ready to be a light for Christ? Pray for God's help. In all that you do, in your words and actions, you give witness to the gospel. God wants you to use all of your gifts to help build up the Church.

I REFLECT

In a 1992 message to young people in the United States, Blessed Mother Teresa encouraged them to exuberantly live out their faith. She said, "May the Immaculate Heart of Mary guide and . . . lead each one of you to respond to Christ's call with your youthful courage and enthusiasm, that you may be true carriers of God's love in the world."

How can you be a true carrier of God's love to the world? Can you start in your own family?

I PRAY

Dear Lord, Jesus, strengthen me in all the gifts of the Holy Spirit so I can be a brilliant light for You. Dear Mother Mary, be at my side and guide me always. Angels and saints, please pray for me. Amen.

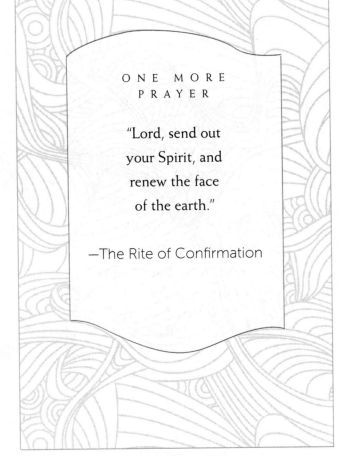

ONE MORE
PRAYER

"Lord, send out
your Spirit, and
renew the face
of the earth."

—The Rite of Confirmation

Acknowledgments

With a grateful heart to the all who have guided me, prayed for me, and loved me throughout my life, my family and friends, especially my parents, Eugene Joseph and Alexandra Mary Cooper, and my brothers and sisters: Alice Jean, Gene, Gary, Barbara, Tim, Michael, and David, I am eternally indebted.

My children: Justin, Chaldea, Jessica, Joseph, and Mary-Catherine—I love you! My husband, David, the wind beneath my wings, thank you for your love and support! Sincere thanks to Jon M. Sweeney and the team at Paraclete Press for their partnership in creating this book.

About the Author

Donna-Marie Cooper O'Boyle is a Catholic wife and mother of five children. Host and creator of EWTN's TV series "Everyday Blessings for Catholic Moms," and "Catholic Mom's Cafe," she's been a Catechist for over twenty-five years, an internationally known speaker, an award-winning journalist, and the best-selling author of numerous Catholic books including: *Catholic Prayer Book for Mothers, The Domestic Church: Room by Room, Grace Café: Serving Up Recipes for Faithful Mothering, Mother Teresa and Me: Ten Years of Friendship, Catholic Saints Prayer Book, The Heart of Motherhood, Prayerfully Expecting: A Nine Month Novena for Mothers to Be, A Catholic Woman's Book of Prayers, Rooted in Love: Our Calling as Catholic Women, Bringing Lent Home with Mother Teresa,*

Embracing Motherhood, and *Catholic Mom's Café: 5-minute Retreats for Every Day of the Year*. Learn more at www. donnacooperoboyle.com

ABOUT PARACLETE PRESS

As the publishing arm of the Community of Jesus, Paraclete Press presents a full expression of Christian belief and practice—from Catholic to Evangelical, from Protestant to Orthodox, reflecting the ecumenical charism of the Community and its dedication to sacred music, the fine arts, and the written word. We publish books, recordings, sheet music, and DVDs that nourish the vibrant life of the church and its people.

WHAT WE ARE DOING

Books

PARACLETE PRESS BOOKS show the richness and depth of what it means to be Christian. While Benedictine spirituality is at the heart of who we are and all that we do, our books reflect the Christian experience across many cultures, time periods, and houses of worship.

We have many series, including *Paraclete Essentials; Paraclete Fiction; Paraclete Giants;* and the new *The Essentials of...*, devoted to Christian classics. Others include *Voices from the Monastery* (men and women monastics writing about living a spiritual life today), *Active Prayer*, the award-winning *Paraclete Poetry*, and new for young readers: *The Pope's Cat*. We also specialize in gift books for children on the occasions of Baptism and First Communion, as well as other important times in a child's life, and books that bring creativity and liveliness to any adult spiritual life.

The MOUNT TABOR BOOKS series focuses on the arts and literature as well as liturgical worship and spirituality; it was created in conjunction with the Mount Tabor Ecumenical Centre for Art and Spirituality in Barga, Italy.

Music

The PARACLETE RECORDINGS label represents the internationally acclaimed choir *Gloriæ Dei Cantores*, the *Gloriæ Dei Cantores* scholas, and the other instrumental artists of the *Arts Empowering Life Foundation.*

Paraclete Press is the exclusive North American distributor for the Gregorian chant recordings from St. Peter's Abbey in Solesmes, France. Paraclete also carries all of the Solesmes chant publications for Mass and the Divine Office, as well as their academic research publications.

In addition, PARACLETE PRESS SHEET MUSIC publishes the work of today's finest composers of sacred choral music, annually reviewing over 1,000 works and releasing between 40 and 60 works for both choir and organ.

Video

Our DVDs offer spiritual help, healing, and biblical guidance for a broad range of life issues including grief and loss, marriage, forgiveness, facing death, understanding suicide, bullying, addictions, Alzheimer's, and Christian formation.

Learn more about us at our website:
www.paracletepress.com
or phone us toll-free at 1.800.451.5006

SCAN
TO
READ
MORE

You may also be interested in . . .

Becoming a Great Godparent
By the editors of Paraclete Press

The perfect combination of gift book and guide for every man or woman asked to take on this enormous and blessed responsibility. Lively, informative, and easy-to-read, this book explains who is eligible to be a godparent and how to be a great one. It offers a brief history of godparenting and reflects on how the whole parish remains involved. It gives suggested prayers and blessings for you and your godchild. And it concludes by answering four commonly asked questions, such as "What if I disagree with how the parents are raising my godchild—should I say something?" and "I am a sincere Protestant Christian believer. Why can't I be the godparent to the child of my best friends, who are Catholic?"

$16.99 | Hardcover | ISBN 978-1-61261-363-5

You may also be interested in . . .

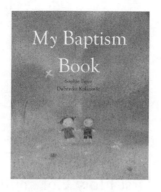

My Baptism Book
By Sophie Piper

Baptism is one of the most important events in a child's life, and *My Baptism Book* is a perfect gift to mark the occasion. Gentle, enchanting illustrations bring to life the simple teachings about God, Jesus, and the Holy Spirit that are appropriate for the youngest of children.

- Brief, meaningful prayers, poems, scriptures, and blessings
- Baptism Gift inscription page and ribbon marker

The message of *My Baptism Book* is one of God's eternal love and care. It is a perfect baptism gift for ages 0–8 and is a popular and well-loved choice.

$14.99 | Jacketed hardcover with ribbon marker
ISBN 978-1-55725-535-8

Also available . . .

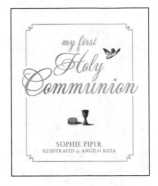

My First Holy Communion
By Sophie Piper

A perfect gift and lasting keepsake, *My First Holy Communion* has the color illustration and textual simplicity to appeal to children, and the charm and respectfulness that adults will appreciate. Ages 7–9.

- Commemoration page and space for photos
- Prayers and Blessings for praising God, remembering Baptism, coming to Confession and living a Christian life
- Helps children understand the significance of taking part in Holy Communion

$14.99 | Jacketed hardcover with ribbon marker
ISBN 978-1-55725-696-6

Available from most booksellers or through Paraclete Press:
www.paracletepress.com; 1-800-451-5006.